ARTISAN Jewelry

Showcase your artistic side with these 9 crocheted accessories. Worked in size 10 Bedspread Weight thread, these easy designs feature earrings, necklaces, and bracelets. Simple jewelry techniques allow you to give each piece a professional finish.

LEISURE ARTS, INC.
Maumelle, Arkansas

TABLE OF CONTENTS

Beaded
NECKLACE & BRACELET

Seed beads add a touch of glam to this easy collar-style necklace and bracelet set. Each closes with buttons and integral button loops. The small size necklace as shown sits close to the neck. For larger necks or for a more relaxed fit, choose one of the larger sizes in parentheses. The bracelet can be adjusted by choosing the correct size then fine-tuning the fit with button placement.

EASY

SHOPPING LIST

Thread (Lace Weight) LACE 0
[350 yards (320 meters) per ball]:

☐ Teal - 1 ball
☐ Lt Green - 1 ball

Steel Crochet Hook

☐ Size 2 (2.25 mm)

Additional Supplies

☐ Size 8/0 glass seed beads - 80{90-100} for Necklace 42{48-54} for Bracelet
☐ Flexible wire beading needle
☐ ½" (12 mm) Button - 1 (for Necklace)
☐ ¼" (6 mm) Button - 2 (for Bracelet)
☐ Sewing needle and matching thread

SIZE INFORMATION

Sizes: Small{Medium-Large}
Necklace: 1¼" wide x 13{15-17}" circumference/3 cm x 33{38-43} cm
Bracelet: 1" wide x 7½{8¼-9¼}" circumference/2.5 cm x 19{21-23.5} cm

Size Note: We have printed the instructions for the sizes in different colors to make it easier for you to find:

- size Small in Blue
- size Medium in Pink
- size Large in Green

Instructions in Black apply to all sizes.

GAUGE INFORMATION

30 sc = 4" (10 cm)
Gauge is not crucial in this project.

NECKLACE

Using beading needle *(Figs. 3a & b, page 46)*, thread 80{90-100} beads onto Lt Green thread and set aside.

With Teal, ch 104{116-128}.

Row 1 (Right side)**:** Working in back ridge of chs *(Fig. 1, page 45)*, sc in sixth ch from hook **(button loop made)** and in each ch across: 99{111-123} sc.

Row 2: Ch 1, turn; sc in first 3 sc, ★ ch 3, skip next 3 sc, sc in next 3 sc; repeat from ★ across: 51{57-63} sc and 16{18-20} ch-3 sps.

Row 3: Ch 1, turn; sc in first 3 sc, ★ ch 4, skip next ch-3 sp, sc in next 3 sc; repeat from ★ across.

Row 4: Ch 1, turn; sc in first 3 sc, ★ ch 5, skip next ch-4 sp, sc in next 3 sc; repeat from ★ across.

Row 5: Ch 1, turn; sc in first 3 sc, ★ ch 6, skip next ch-5 sp, sc in next 3 sc; repeat from ★ across.

Row 6: Ch 1, turn; sc in first 3 sc, ★ ch 7, skip next ch-6 sp, sc in next 3 sc; repeat from ★ across changing to Lt Green in last sc *(Fig. A)*; cut Teal.

Fig. A

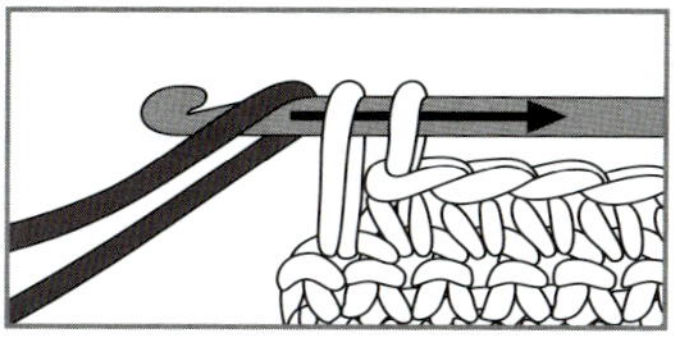

Row 7: With Lt Green, ch 1, turn; sc in first 3 sc, ★ ch 8, skip next ch-7 sp, sc in next 3 sc; repeat from ★ across.

Row 8: Ch 1, turn; sc in first 3 sc, ★ ch 2, (ch around bead) 5 times *(Figs. 2a-d, page 45)*, ch 2, skip next ch-8 sp, sc in next 3 sc; repeat from ★ across; finish off.

Sew button opposite button loop.

BRACELET

Using beading needle, thread 21{24-27} beads onto Lt Green.

Foundation Ch: With Lt Green, ch 4, (ch around bead) 3 times, ★ ch 5, (ch around bead) 3 times; repeat from ★ 5{6-7} times **more**, ch 8: 21{24-27} chs around beads and 42{47-52} chs.

Row 1: Working in back ridge of chs, sc in fifth ch from hook (**button loop made**) and in next 2 chs, ★ ch 3, skip next 5 chs, sc in next 3 chs; repeat from ★ across changing to Teal in last sc; cut Lt Green: 24{27-30} sc, 7{8-9} ch-3 sps, and one button loop.

Rows 2 and 3: With Teal, ch 1, turn; sc in first 3 sc, ★ ch 3, skip next ch-3 sp, sc in next 3 sc; repeat from ★ across.

Row 4 (Right side)**:** Ch 1, turn; sc in first 3 sc, ★ ch 3, skip next ch-3 sp, sc in next 3 sc; repeat from ★ across; finish off.

Using beading needle, thread 21{24-27} beads onto Lt Green.

Row 5: With **right** side facing, join Lt Green with sc in first sc ***(see Joining With Sc, page 45)***; sc in next 2 sc, ★ ch 3, skip next ch-3 sp, sc in next 3 sc; repeat from ★ across.

Row 6: Ch 4 (**button loop made**), turn; sc in first 3 sc, ★ ch 1, (ch around bead) 3 times, ch 1, skip next ch-3 sp, sc in next 3 sc; repeat from ★ across; finish off.

Try on bracelet and sew buttons opposite button loops, adjusting to fit. (Buttons can be made using additional beads if desired).

CHAIN LINK
Necklace

CHAIN LINK
Necklace

You'll quickly memorize the instructions for this fun and easy necklace. Use the elegant colors shown here or choose colors to match your outfit. It's a great way to use up odd bits and pieces of thread. You may find it easier to weave in ends as you work each link, rather than waiting until all the links are complete. The necklace shown has about a 23" (58.5 cm) circumference, but you can easily customize it to your preferred length; just make sure it's long enough to fit over your head!

Finished Size: 23" (58.5 cm) circumference

EASY

SHOPPING LIST

Thread (Lace Weight) LACE 0

[350 yards (320 meters) per ball]:

☐ Burgundy - 1 ball

[100 yards (91.5 meters) per ball]:

☐ Gold - 1 ball

Note: It takes approximately 1½ yards (1.4 meters) to crochet one Link

Steel Crochet Hook

☐ Size 2 (2.25 mm)

Gauge is not crucial in this project.

NECKLACE

First Link

With Gold, ch 10; join with slip st to form a ring.

Rnd 1 (Right side)**:** Ch 1, 20 sc in ring; join with slip st to first sc, finish off.

Second Link

With Burgundy, ch 10, insert thread tail from **wrong** side to **right** side through center of previous Link; join with slip st to form a ring.

Rnd 1 (Right side)**:** Ch 1, 20 sc in ring; join with slip st to first sc, finish off.

Third Link

With Gold, ch 10, insert thread tail from **wrong** side to **right** side through center of previous Link; join with slip st to form a ring.

Rnd 1 (Right side)**:** Ch 1, 20 sc in ring; join with slip st to first sc, finish off.

The **right** side of the Links should each face the same way throughout.

Repeat Second and Third Links, 22 times: 47 Links total.

Last Link

With Burgundy, ch 10, insert thread tail from **right** side to **wrong** side through center of previous Link **and** from **wrong** side to **right** side through center of First Link; join with slip st to form a ring.

Rnd 1 (Right side)**:** Ch 1, 20 sc in ring; join with slip st to first sc, finish off.

ZIG-ZAG Bracelet

Take a twist and take a turn to crochet this colorful cuff-style bracelet. The color work stitches create a flower-like motif that could also appear as diamonds in a different colorway. Shown in pink and golden tones, this bracelet would be just as pretty in black and white or in tone-on-tone colors, like teal and aqua. Change the look from fun and fanciful to charming and sophisticated just by swapping out the flower button to a jeweled fastener.

Finished Size:

1" wide x 7½" long (2.5 cm x 19 cm)

EASY

SHOPPING LIST

Thread (Lace Weight) LACE 0

[350 yards (320 meters) per ball]:

- ☐ Pink - 1 ball
- ☐ Yellow - 1 ball

Steel Crochet Hook

- ☐ Size 2 (2.25 mm)

Additional Supplies

- ☐ Safety pin - 1
- ☐ ½" (12 mm) Button - 1
- ☐ Sewing needle and matching thread

GAUGE INFORMATION

28 sc = 4" (10 cm)

BRACELET

With Pink, ch 48.

Row 1 (Right side)**:** Working in back ridge of chs *(Fig. 1, page 45)*, sc in second ch from hook and in each ch across: 47 sc.

Note: Loop a short piece of thread around any stitch on Row 1 to mark **right** side.

Row 2: Ch 1, turn; sc in first 2 sc, ★ ch 1, skip next sc, sc in next 2 sc; repeat from ★ across changing to Yellow in last sc *(Fig. A)*; cut Pink: 32 sc and 15 ch-1 sps.

Fig. A

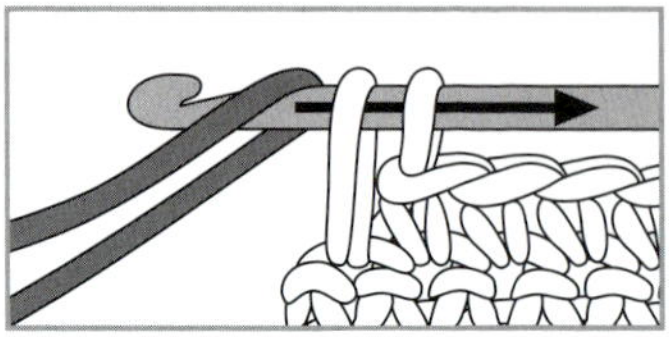

Row 3: With Yellow, ch 3 **(counts as first dc, now and throughout)**, turn; (dc, ch 1, dc) in each ch-1 sp across to last 2 sc, skip next sc, dc in last sc changing to Pink *(Fig. B)*; do **not** cut Yellow.

Fig. B

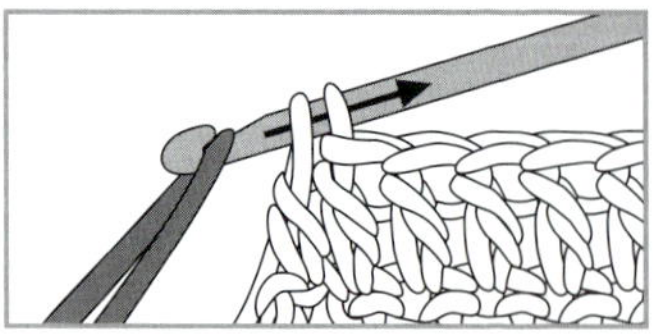

Row 4: With Pink, ch 2 **(counts as first hdc)**, turn; (dc, ch 1, dc) in each ch-1 sp across to last 2 dc, skip next dc, hdc in last dc; place loop from hook onto safety pin while you work the next row.

Row 5: With **wrong** side facing, insert hook in first hdc on Row 4, YO with Yellow and pull up a loop, ch 1 **loosely**; working **around** sts on Row 4 ***(Fig. C)***, (dc, ch 1, dc) in sp **between** first and second dc on Row 3 ***(Fig. D)***, ★ skip next ch-1 sp on Row 3, (dc, ch 1, dc) in sp **between** next 2 dc on Row 3; repeat from ★ across; finish off Yellow, remove safety pin and place Pink loop on hook: 32 dc and 16 ch-1 sps.

Fig. C

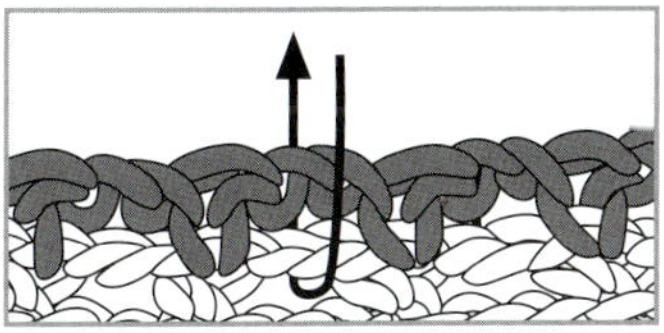

Fig. D

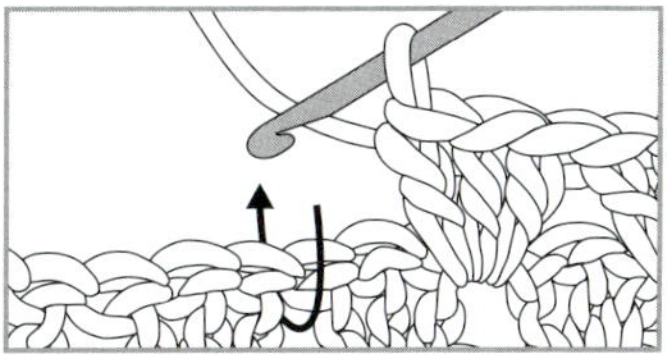

Row 6: With Pink, ch 1, turn; sc in first dc and in next ch-1 sp, sc in sp **between** next 2 dc, ★ sc in next dc and in next ch-1 sp, sc in sp **between** next 2 dc; repeat from ★ across to last ch-1 sp, sc in last ch-1 sp and last dc: 47 sc.

Row 7: Ch 1, turn; sc in each sc across; do **not** finish off.

Button Band

Row 1: Ch 1,do **not** turn; work 8 sc evenly spaced across end of rows: 8 sc.

Row 2 (Right side)**:** Ch 1, turn; sc in each sc across; finish off.

Buttonhole Band

Row 1: With **right** facing and working in end of rows opposite Button Band, join Pink with sc in first row ***(see Joining With Sc, page 45)***; work 7 sc evenly spaced across: 8 sc.

Row 2: Ch 1, turn; sc in first 3 sc, ch 2, skip next 2 sc **(buttonhole made)**, sc in last 3 sc: 6 sc and one ch-2 sp.

Row 3: Ch 1, turn; sc in first 3 sc, 2 sc in next ch-2 sp, sc in last 3 sc; finish off.

Sew on button opposite buttonhole, adjusting placement for best fit.

Flower
CUFF & EARRINGS

Flower
CUFF & EARRINGS

A cascade of tiny flowers covers this button-on cuff. Use all your brightly colored leftover threads, as each flower takes only a small amount of thread. Be sure to leave the tails on the petal colors long enough to sew the flowers onto the cuff. Create the matching earrings using your choice of colors.

Finished Size:

Approximately 1½" wide x 8¼" long (4 cm x 21 cm)

EASY

SHOPPING LIST

Thread (Lace Weight) LACE 0
[350 yards (320 meters) per ball]:

- ☐ Olive - 1 ball
- ☐ Orange - 1 ball
- ☐ Yellow - 1 ball
- ☐ Pink - 1 ball
- ☐ Lavender - 1 ball

Steel Crochet Hook

- ☐ Size 2 (2.25 mm) **and** Size 10 (1.3 mm)

Additional Supplies

- ☐ ½" (12 mm) Buttons - 2 (for Cuff)
- ☐ Fishhook ear wires - 2
- ☐ Tapestry needle
- ☐ Sewing needle and matching thread

GAUGE INFORMATION

With size 2 hook,
28 dc = 4" (10 cm)

Use size 2 hook throughout, unless otherwise indicated.

CUFF

With Olive, ch 60.

Row 1: Working in back ridge of chs *(Fig. 1, page 45)*, dc in fourth ch from hook **(3 skipped chs count as first dc)** and in each ch across: 58 dc.

Row 2 (Right side)**:** Ch 3 **(counts as first dc, now and throughout)**, turn; dc in next dc and in each dc to last 4 dc, ch 1, skip next dc **(buttonhole made)**, dc in last 3 dc: 57 dc and one ch-1 sp.

Row 3: Ch 3, turn; dc in next dc and in each dc and ch-1 sp across: 58 dc.

Rows 4 and 5: Repeat Rows 2 and 3.

Finish off.

Flowers

Using remaining colors, make approximately 25 flowers in a variety of colors and shapes, as follows:

FLOWER 1

With center color, ch 5; join with slip st to form a ring.

Rnd 1 (Right side)**:** Ch 1, 6 sc in ring; join with slip st to first sc, finish off.

Rnd 2: With **right** side facing, join petal color with slip st in any sc; (ch 3, dc, ch 3, slip st) in same st, (slip st, ch 3, dc, ch 3, slip st) in each sc around; finish off leaving a long end for sewing.

FLOWER 2

With desired color, ch 15.

Row 1: 3 Sc in second ch from hook, 2 hdc in each ch across; finish off leaving a long end for sewing.

Arrange into a spiral flower shape with sc end in the center. Use long end to sew through layers of spiral to maintain shape.

For additional flowers, vary the length of the beginning ch, from 15 to 20 chs, to change the size of the flower.

FLOWER 3

With center color, ch 5; join with slip st to form a ring.

Rnd 1 (Right side)**:** Ch 1, 6 sc in ring; join with slip st to first sc, finish off.

Rnd 2: With **right** side facing, join petal color with slip st in any sc; (ch 3, slip st in next sc) around; finish off.

Finishing

Sew on buttons opposite buttonholes, adjusting placement for best fit.
Using photo, page 17, as a guide for placement, sew Flowers to Cuff.

EARRINGS

First Earring

LARGER FLOWER

With desired colors, make Cuff Flower 1.

SMALLER FLOWER

Rnd 1 (Right side)**:** With center color and size 10 hook, work same as Cuff Flower 1: 6 sc.

Rnd 2: With **right** side facing and using size 10 hook, join petal color with slip st in any sc; ★ (ch 3, dc, ch 3, slip st) in same st, slip st in next sc; repeat from ★ 4 times **more**, ch 3, dc in same st; with **right** side facing, slip st in center dc of any petal on Larger Flower, ch 3, slip st in same st on Smaller Flower; finish off.

Attach ear wire to Larger Flower.

Second Earring

Using size 10 hook and desired colors, make Cuff Flower 1.

Attach ear wire to Flower.

CIRCLES & BEADS
Necklace

Incredibly easy crocheting in a bright multicolored thread makes this a perfect project for all ages. Make as many crocheted circles as you choose, and have fun picking matching beads to use as spacers. String them all onto a simple suede cord, and you're all set.

Finished Size:

Approximately 40" (101.5 cm) circumference

EASY

SHOPPING LIST

Thread (Lace Weight) LACE 0
[350 yards (320 meters) per ball]:
- ☐ 1 ball

Steel Crochet Hook
- ☐ Size 2 (2.25 mm)

Additional Supplies
- ☐ 40" (101.5 cm) length Suede lace cord
- ☐ 8 mm silver spacer - 30 beads with large holes
- ☐ Fold-over cord ends - 2
- ☐ Craft glue
- ☐ Jump rings - 2
- ☐ Lobster clasp - 1
- ☐ Chain-nose pliers (2 pair)

GAUGE INFORMATION

Each Circle Motif = 7/8" (2 cm) diameter

Gauge is not crucial in this project.

CIRCLE MOTIF
(Make 25)

Ch 6; join with slip st to form a ring.

Rnd 1 (Right side)**:** Ch 3 **(counts as first dc)**, 15 dc in ring; join with slip st to first dc, finish off.

FINISHING

Thread 3 beads onto cord; then alternately thread one circle motif and one bead, ending with 3 beads following last motif.

Lay one suede end in one fold-over cord end, apply a drop of glue, and use the chain-nose pliers to fold the tabs down over the suede end ***(Fig. A)***.

Repeat with the opposite end of the suede. Join one jump ring and lobster clasp to one fold-over cord end and the remaining jump ring to the other fold-over cord end.

Fig. A

Motif
NECKLACE & EARRINGS

Motif
NECKLACE & EARRINGS

A cascade of flower-inspired motifs heralds spring! Using the join-as-you-go method makes putting the puzzle pieces together a breeze. You'll want to use the stitch chart provided to help you understand where the motifs fit together. You might even get carried away and create additional motifs to make a freeform-style necklace.

Finished Size:

20½" (52 cm) circumference

EASY +

SHOPPING LIST

Thread (Lace Weight) LACE 0
[350 yards (320 meters) per ball]:
- ☐ Lavender - 1 ball
- ☐ Lt Green - 1 ball

Steel Crochet Hook
- ☐ Size 2 (2.25 mm) **and** Size 10 (1.3 mm)

Additional Supplies
- ☐ ½" (12 mm) diameter Button - 1 (for Necklace)
- ☐ Fishhook ear wire - 2
- ☐ Sewing needle and matching thread

Gauge is not crucial in this project.

STITCH GUIDE

2-DC CLUSTER (uses one sp)
★ YO, insert hook in sp indicated, YO and pull up a loop, YO and draw through 2 loops on hook; repeat from ★ once **more**, YO and draw through all 3 loops on hook.

3-DC CLUSTER (uses one sp)
★ YO, insert hook in sp indicated, YO and pull up a loop, YO and draw through 2 loops on hook; repeat from ★ 2 time **more**, YO and draw through all 4 loops on hook.

PICOT
Ch 3, slip st in top of last Cluster made.

BACK POST DOUBLE CROCHET *(abbreviated BPdc)*
YO, insert hook from **back** to **front** around post of dc indicated *(Fig. A)*, YO and pull up a loop (3 loops on hook), (YO and draw through 2 loops on hook) twice.

Fig. A

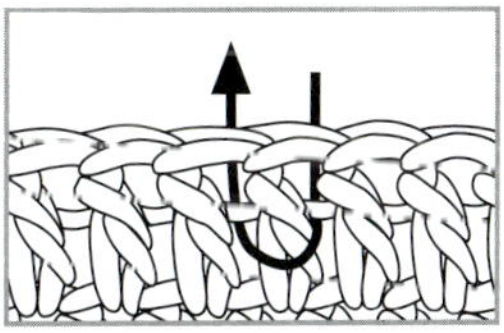

NECKLACE

Use size 2 hook throughout.

Center Motif

With Lt Green, ch 5; join with slip st to form a ring.

Rnd 1 (Right side)**:** Ch 3 **(counts as first dc, now and throughout)**, 11 dc in ring; join with slip st to first dc, finish off: 12 dc.

Note: Loop a short piece of thread around any stitch to mark Rnd 1 as **right** side.

Rnd 2: With **right** side facing, join Lavender with sc in any dc ***(see Joining With Sc, page 45)***; ch 7, sc in same st, ch 1, skip next dc, ★ (sc, ch 7, sc) in next dc, ch 1, skip next dc; repeat from ★ around; join with slip st to first sc: 6 ch-7 sps.

Rnd 3: Ch 1, in each ch-7 sp work (sc, 2 hdc, 3 dc, ch 2, 3 dc, 2 hdc, sc); join with slip st to first sc, finish off: 6 petals.

First Side

SIDE MOTIF

With Lavender, ch 5; join with slip st to form a ring.

Rnd 1 (Right side)**:** Ch 4 **(counts as first dc plus ch 1)**, (dc in ring, ch 1) 11 times; join with slip st to first dc, finish off: 12 dc and 12 ch-1 sps.

Note: Mark Rnd 1 as **right** side.

Rnd 2: With **right** side facing, join Lt Green with dc in any ch-1 sp ***(see Joining With Dc, page 45)***; ch 3, work 3-dc Cluster in next ch-1 sp, ★ work Picot, ch 3, dc in next dc, ch 3, work 3-dc Cluster in next ch-1 sp; repeat from ★ 4 times **more**; ch 1, with **right** side of Center Motif facing, slip st in any ch-2 sp, ch 1, slip st in top of last Cluster made, ch 3; join with slip st to first dc, finish off.

SMALL MOTIF #1

With Lavender, ch 6; join with slip st to form a ring.

Rnd 1 (Right side)**:** Ch 2, work 2-dc Cluster in ring, ★ ch 5, slip st in third ch from hook, ch 2, work 3-dc Cluster in ring; repeat from ★ 4 times **more**; ch 3, with **right** side of Side Motif facing, slip st in Picot indicated on Placement Diagram, ch 1, slip st in ch before slip st just made, ch 2; skip beginning ch-2 and join with slip st to top of first Cluster, finish off.

PLACEMENT DIAGRAM

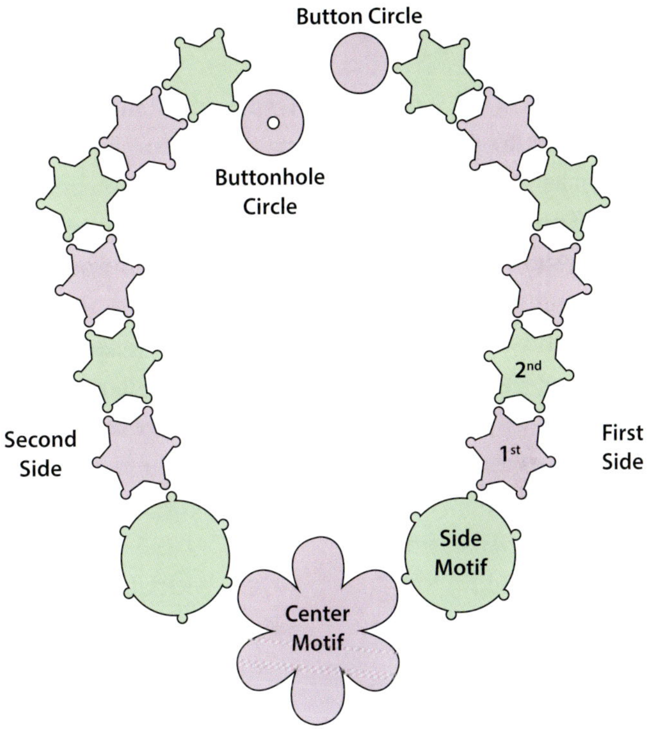

Continue referring to Placement Diagram to join remaining Motifs.

SMALL MOTIF #2

With Lt Green, ch 6; join with slip st to form a ring.

Rnd 1 (Right side)**:** Ch 2, work 2-dc Cluster in ring, ★ ch 5, slip st in third ch from hook, ch 2, work 3-dc Cluster in ring; repeat from ★ 3 times **more**; ch 3, with **right** side of **previous** Motif facing, slip st in Picot indicated on Diagram, ch 1, slip st in ch before slip st just made, ch 2, work 3-dc Cluster in ring, ch 3, slip st in next Picot on **previous** Motif, ch 1, slip st in ch before slip st just made, ch 2; skip beginning ch-2 and join with slip st to top of first Cluster, finish off.

Alternating Lavender and Lt Green, work Small Motif #2, 4 times **more**.

BUTTON CIRCLE

With Lavender, ch 4; join with slip st to form a ring.

Rnd 1 (Right side)**:** Ch 3, 9 dc in ring, with **right** side of **previous** Motif facing, slip st in Picot indicated on Diagram, 2 dc in ring; join with slip st to first dc, finish off: 16 dc.

Second Side

Skipping next ch-2 sp on Center Motif, work same as First Side to Button Circle.

BUTTONHOLE CIRCLE

With Lavender, ch 6; join with slip st to form a ring (**buttonhole made**).

Rnd 1 (Right side)**:** Ch 3, 14 dc in ring, with **right** side of **previous** Motif facing, slip st in Picot indicated on Diagram, dc in ring; join with slip st to first dc; finish off: 16 dc.

Sew button to Button Circle.

EARRING (Make 2)

With Lavender, ch 5; join with slip st to form a ring.

Rnd 1 (Right side)**:** Ch 3, 11 dc in ring; join with slip st to first dc, finish off: 12 dc.

Note: Mark Rnd 1 as **right** side.

Rnd 2: With **right** side facing, join Lt Green with BPdc around any dc; ch 1, (work BPdc around next dc, ch 1) around; join with slip st to first BPdc, finish off.

Rnd 3: With **right** side facing, join Lavender with sc in any ch-1 sp ***(see Joining With Sc, page 45)***; ch 3, sc in same sp, (sc, ch 3, sc) in each ch-1 sp around; join with slip st to first sc, finish off.

Attach an ear wire to each Motif.

Woven BRACELET

Woven
BRACELET

A double crochet mesh serves as the warp for this woven-look bracelet. Take care not to tie the weaving strands too tightly. To adjust the size of the bracelet, add or subtract a multiple of 4 to the beginning chain.

Finished Size:

1" wide x 7" circumference (2.5 cm x 18 cm)

EASY

SHOPPING LIST

Thread (Lace Weight) LACE 0
[350 yards (320 meters) per ball]:
- ☐ Purple -1 ball
- ☐ Orange - 2½ yards (2.3 meters)
- ☐ Aqua - 2½ yards (2.3 meters)
- ☐ Yellow - 2½ yards (2.3 meters)
- ☐ Pink - 2½ yards (2.3 meters)

Steel Crochet Hook
- ☐ Size 2 (2.25 mm)

GAUGE INFORMATION

23 sts = 3" (7.5 cm)

BAND

With Purple, ch 56; being careful **not** to twist ch, join with slip st to back ridge of first ch to form a ring *(Fig. 1, page 45)*.

Rnd 1 (Right side)**:** Ch 4 **(counts as first dc plus ch 1, now and throughout)**, skip next ch, ★ dc in back ridge of next ch, ch 1, skip next ch; repeat from ★ around; join with slip st to first dc: 28 ch-1 sps.

Rnds 2-4: Ch 4, (dc in next dc, ch 1) around; join with slip st to first dc.

Finish off.

Cut six 14" (35.5 cm) strands of Orange. Holding strands together, weave through ch-1 sps of Rnd 1. Holding cut ends of strands together, tie ends in an overhand knot close to bracelet *(Fig. 4, page 46)*; trim as desired.

Repeat with Aqua, Yellow, and Pink, weaving through sps of Rnds 2-4.

FAN Pendant

A few beads and a few yards of thread create this simple layered pendant. A chain link necklace finishes off the look. Fancy it up even more by adding more beads throughout, or by adding additional fans along a crocheted cord.

Finished Size:

Approximately 3" wide x 2" long (7.5 cm x 5 cm) not including chain

EASY

SHOPPING LIST

Thread (Lace Weight) LACE 0
[350 yards (320 meters) per ball]:

- ☐ Blue - 1 ball
- ☐ Lt Green - 1 ball

Steel Crochet Hook

- ☐ Size 2 (2.25 mm)

Additional Supplies

- ☐ Size 8/0 glass seed beads - 21
- ☐ Flexible wire beading needle
- ☐ Pinch bail - 1
- ☐ Small link chain (desired length)
- ☐ Jump rings - 2
- ☐ Lobster clasp - 1
- ☐ Chain-nose pliers - 2 pair

Gauge is not crucial in this project.

PENDANT

Large Fan

Using beading needle *(Figs. 3a & b, page 46)*, thread 14 beads onto Blue thread.

Row 1: Ch 8 **(counts as first dc plus ch 5)**, dc in eighth ch from hook: 2 dc and one ch-5 sp.

Row 2 (Right side)**:** Ch 3 **(counts as first dc, now and throughout)**, turn; 5 dc in next ch-5 sp, dc in last dc: 7 dc.

Row 3: Ch 5 **(counts as first dc plus ch 2)**, turn; dc in next dc, (ch 2, dc in next dc) across: 7 dc and 6 ch-2 sps.

Row 4: Ch 6 **(counts as first dc plus ch 3)**, turn; (dc in next ch-2 sp, ch 3) across, dc in last dc: 8 dc and 7 ch-3 sps.

Row 5: Ch 3, turn; 2 dc in next ch-3 sp, (ch 1, 2 dc in next ch-3 sp) across, dc in last dc: 16 dc and 6 ch-1 sps.

Row 6: Ch 4 **(counts as first dc plus ch 1)**, turn; (dc, ch 1) twice in each ch-1 sp across to last 3 dc, skip next 2 dc, dc in last dc: 14 dc and 13 ch-1 sps.

Row 7: Ch 1, turn; sc in first dc, ch 1, ch around bead ***(Figs. 2a-d, page 45)***, ch 1, ★ sc in next ch-1 sp, ch 1, ch around bead, ch 1; repeat from ★ across to last dc, sc in last dc, finish off.

Small Fan

Using beading needle, thread 7 beads onto Lt Green thread.

Rows 1-3: Work same as Large Fan: 7 dc and 6 ch-2 sps.

Row 4: Ch 4, turn; ch around bead, ch 1, ★ dc in next ch-2 sp, ch 1, ch around bead, ch 1; repeat from ★ across to last dc, dc in last dc; finish off.

Place **wrong** side of Small Fan on top of **right** side of Large Fan. Attach pinch bail around both loops of Fans. Attach lobster clasp to one end of chain length with jump ring. Attach remaining jump ring to opposite end of chain. Thread chain through pinch bail.

Bead
& TASSEL PENDANT

This pendant offers lots of opportunity for experimentation. Change up the basic pattern by switching colors, adding multiple beads and/or purchased tassels. Try hanging it from a colorful ribbon. Options abound!

Finished Size:

Approximately 2½" (6.5 cm) diameter

EASY

SHOPPING LIST

Thread (Lace Weight) LACE 0

[350 yards (320 meters) per ball]:

- ☐ Purple - 1 ball
- ☐ Olive - 1 ball
- ☐ Orange - 1 ball

Steel Crochet Hook

- ☐ Size 2 (2.25 mm)

Additional Supplies

- ☐ 1" (25 mm) diameter decorative wooden bead (hole in bead must be large enough to accommodate 6 strands of thread)
- ☐ 18" (45.5 cm) long Suede lace cord
- ☐ Fold-over cord ends - 2
- ☐ Craft glue
- ☐ Lobster clasp
- ☐ 10 mm Jump ring - 1
  6 mm Jump rings - 2
- ☐ Tapestry needle
- ☐ Chain-nose pliers (2 pair)

Gauge is not crucial in this project.

STITCH GUIDE

REVERSE SINGLE CROCHET

Working from **left** to **right**, ★ insert hook in st to right of hook ***(Fig. A)***, YO and draw through, under and to left of loop on hook (2 loops on hook) ***(Fig. B)***, YO and draw through both loops on hook ***(Fig. C)*** **(reverse sc made, *Fig. D*)**; repeat from ★ around.

Fig. A

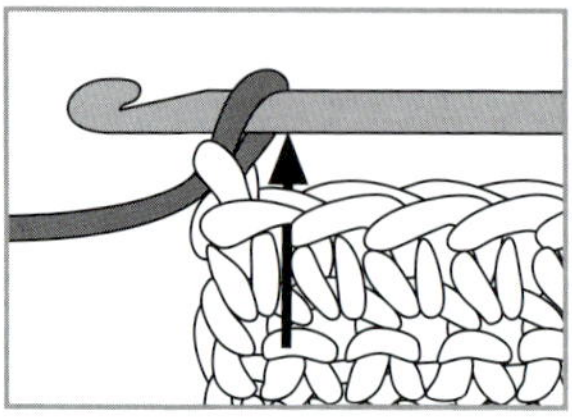

Fig. B

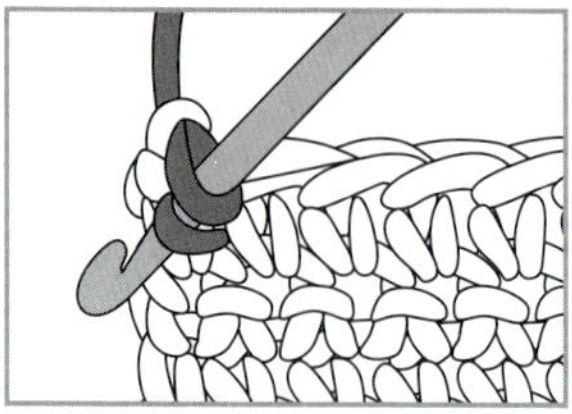

Fig. C

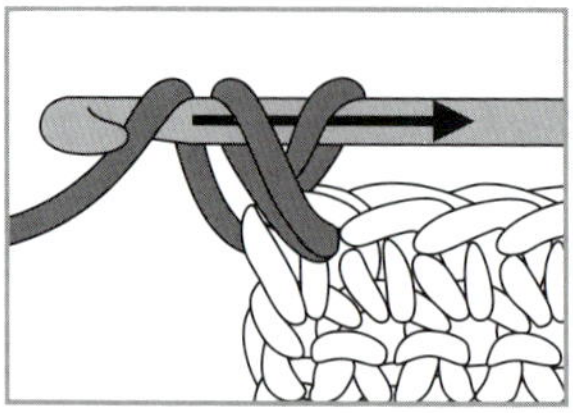

Fig. D

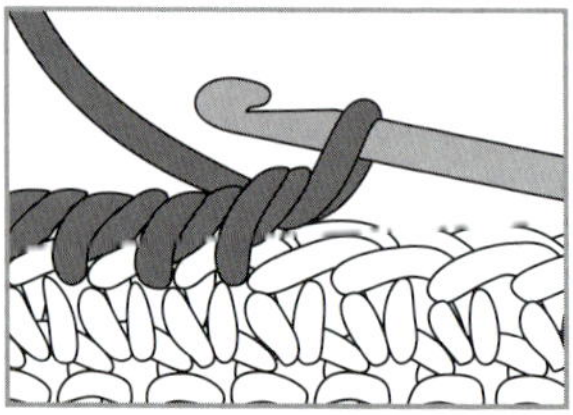

PENDANT

With Olive, ch 4; join with slip st to form a ring.

Rnd 1 (Right side)**:** Ch 3 **(counts as first dc, now and throughout)**, 11 dc in ring; join with slip st to first dc, finish off: 12 dc.

Note: Loop a short piece of thread around any stitch to mark Rnd 1 as **right** side.

Rnd 2: With **right** side facing, join Purple with dc in any dc ***(see Joining With Dc, page 45)***; 2 dc in same st as joining, (ch 1, skip next dc, 3 dc in next dc) 3 times, tie a short piece of thread around last dc made for hanging loop placement, ch 1, skip next dc, 3 dc in next dc, ch 1, skip next dc, dc in next dc, tie a short piece of thread around last dc made for hanging loop placement, 2 dc in same st, ch 1, skip last dc; join with slip st to first dc, finish off: 18 dc and 6 ch-1 sps.

Rnd 3: With **right** side facing, join Olive with dc in first dc of any 3-dc group; 2 dc in next dc, dc in next dc, 3 dc in next ch-1 sp, ★ dc in next dc, 2 dc in next dc, dc in next dc, 3 dc in next ch-1 sp; repeat from ★ around; join with slip st to first dc, finish off: 42 dc.

Rnd 4: With **right** side facing, join Orange with sc in any dc ***(see Joining With Sc, page 45)***; (ch 1, skip next dc, sc in next dc) twice, ch 2, skip next dc, ★ sc in next dc, (ch 1, skip next dc, sc in next dc) twice, ch 2, skip next dc; repeat from ★ around; join with slip st to first sc, finish off: 21 sc and 21 sps.

Rnd 5: With **right** side facing, join Purple with dc in any sp; 2 dc in same sp, 3 dc in each sp around; join with slip st to first sc, do **not** finish off: 63 dc.

Rnd 6: Ch 1, working from **left** to **right**, work reverse sc in each dc around; join with slip st to first sc, finish off.

Hanging Loop

With **wrong** side facing, join Purple with slip st around marked dc, remove marker; ch 6, slip st around next marked dc, remove marker; finish off.

Attach 10 mm jump ring around hanging loop.

Tassel

With **wrong** side facing and Hanging Loop at the top, tie a scrap piece of thread to center st at bottom edge for Tassel placement.

Cut one 12" (30.5 cm) strand **each** of Purple, Olive, and Orange. Holding the 3 strands together and thread strands through marked stitch. Align ends and tie an overhand knot close to the Pendant ***(Fig. 4, page 46)***. Thread these 6 strands through hole in the bead.

Cut two 10" (25.5 cm) strands **each** of Purple, Olive, and Orange. Holding these 6 strands together, tie them around the existing strands at the base of the bead, leaving equal lengths on each side of knot. Tighten knot as much as possible. Smooth cut ends of tassel so that strands are parallel to each other.

Cut one 6" (15 cm) strand of Olive. Holding one end of the strand parallel to tassel, wrap remaining end **tightly** around the knot, securing cut end of strand and covering the knot. Secure end by running it through the knot several times. Cut end close to tassel. Trim tassel ends to 2¾" (7 cm) or to desired length.

Lay one suede end in one fold-over cord end, apply a drop of glue, and use the chain-nose pliers to fold the tabs down over the suede end ***(Fig. A)***.
Repeat with the opposite end of the suede. Join one jump ring and lobster clasp to one fold-over cord end and the remaining jump ring to the other fold-over cord end. Thread cord through 10 mm jump ring.

Fig. A

General Instructions

ABBREVIATIONS

BPdc	Back Post double crochet(s)
ch(s)	chain(s)
cm	centimeters
dc	double crochet(s)
hdc	half double crochet(s)
mm	millimeters
Rnd(s)	Round(s)
sc	single crochet(s)
sp(s)	space(s)
st(s)	stitch(es)
YO	yarn over

SYMBOLS & TERMS

★ — work instructions following ★ as many **more** times as indicated in addition to the first time.

( ) or **[ ]** — work enclosed instructions **as many** times as specified by the number immediately following **or** work all enclosed instructions in the stitch or space indicated **or** contains explanatory remarks.

colon (:) — the number(s) given after a colon at the end of a row or round denote(s) the number of stitches or spaces you should have on that row or round.

CROCHET TERMINOLOGY		
UNITED STATES		INTERNATIONAL
slip stitch (slip st)	=	single crochet (sc)
single crochet (sc)	=	double crochet (dc)
half double crochet (hdc)	=	half treble crochet (htr)
double crochet (dc)	=	treble crochet (tr)
treble crochet (tr)	=	double treble crochet (dtr)
double treble crochet (dtr)	=	triple treble crochet (ttr)
triple treble crochet (tr tr)	=	quadruple treble crochet (qtr)
skip	=	miss

STEEL CROCHET HOOKS																
U.S.	00	0	1	2	3	4	5	6	7	8	9	10	11	12	13	14
Metric - mm	3.5	3.25	2.75	2.25	2.1	2	1.9	1.8	1.65	1.5	1.4	1.3	1.1	1	.85	.75

GAUGE

All of the instructions are written for bedspread weight cotton thread (size 10). Gauge is not important for most of the projects; your project may be a little larger or smaller without changing the overall effect. When a gauge is given in the individual instructions, make a sample swatch in the thread and hook specified. If your swatch is larger or smaller than specified, **make another, changing hook size to get the correct gauge**. Keep trying until you find the size hook that will give you the specified gauge.

BEGINNER	Projects for first-time crocheters using basic stitches. Minimal shaping.
EASY	Projects using yarn with basic stitches, repetitive stitch patterns, simple color changes, and simple shaping and finishing.
INTERMEDIATE	Projects using a variety of techniques, such as basic lace patterns or color patterns, mid-level shaping and finishing.
EXPERIENCED	Projects with intricate stitch patterns, techniques and dimension, such as non-repeating patterns, multi-color techniques, fine threads, small hooks, detailed shaping and refined finishing.

Yarn Weight Symbol & Names	LACE 0	SUPER FINE 1	FINE 2	LIGHT 3	MEDIUM 4	BULKY 5	SUPER BULKY 6	JUMBO 7
Type of Yarns in Category	Fingering, size 10 crochet thread	Sock, Fingering, Baby	Sport, Baby	DK, Light Worsted	Worsted, Afghan, Aran	Chunky, Craft, Rug	Super Bulky, Roving	Jumbo, Roving
Crochet Gauge* Ranges in Single Crochet to 4" (10 cm)	32-42 sts**	21-32 sts	16-20 sts	12-17 sts	11-14 sts	8-11 sts	6-9 sts	5 sts and fewer
Advised Hook Size Range	Steel*** 6 to 8, Regular hook B-1	B-1 to E-4	E-4 to 7	7 to I-9	I-9 to K-10½	K-10½ to M/N-13	M/N-13 to Q	Q and larger

*GUIDELINES ONLY: The chart above reflects the most commonly used gauges and hook sizes for specific yarn categories.

** Lace weight yarns are usually crocheted with larger hooks to create lacy openwork patterns. Accordingly, a gauge range is difficult to determine. Always follow the gauge stated in your pattern.

*** Steel crochet hooks are sized differently from regular hooks–the higher the number, the smaller the hook, which is the reverse of regular hook sizing.

JOINING WITH SC

When instructed to join with sc, begin with a slip knot on the hook. YO, holding loop on hook, insert hook in stitch or space indicated, YO and pull up a loop, YO and draw through both loops on hook.

JOINING WITH DC

When instructed to join with dc, begin with a slip knot on the hook. YO, holding loop on hook, insert hook in stitch or space indicated, YO and pull up a loop (3 loops on hook), (YO and draw through 2 loops on hook) twice.

BACK RIDGE

Work only in loops indicated by arrows *(Fig. 1)*.

Fig. 1

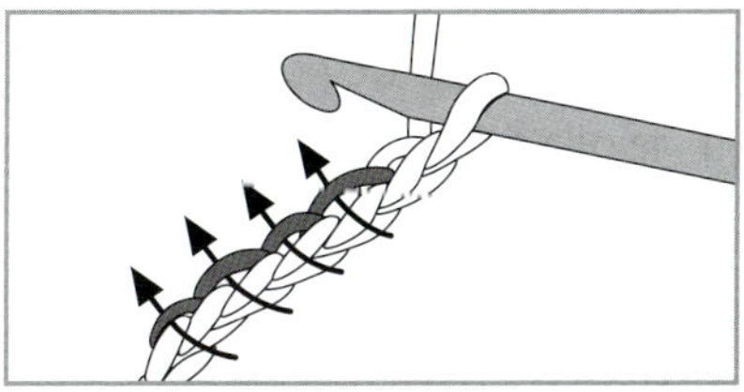

WORK A CHAIN AROUND A BEAD

Slide a bead up against the last chain made *(Fig. 2a)*.

Fig. 2a

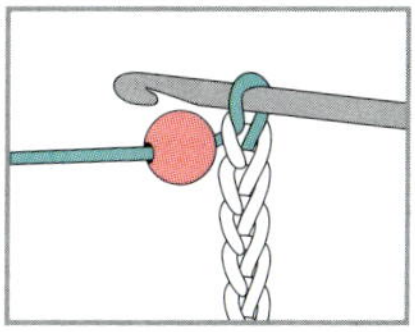

Pull the loop on the hook larger to fit around the bead *(Fig. 2b)*, then YO *(Fig. 2c)* and draw through the loop on the hook to complete the chain *(Fig. 2d)*.

Fig. 2b

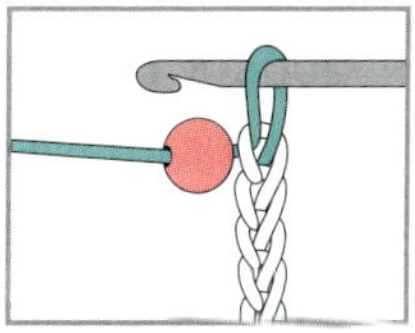

Fig. 2c

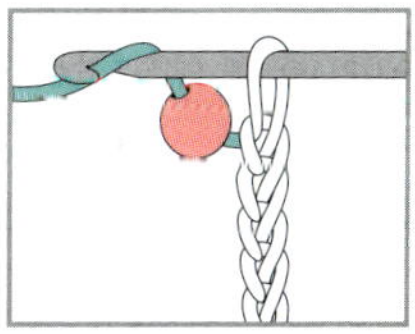

Fig. 2d

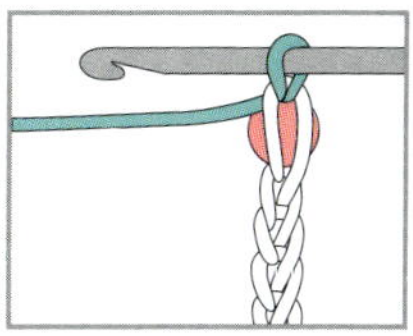

STRINGING BEADS

Thread a flexible wire beading needle with the thread ***(Figs. 3a & b)***, then string the number of beads needed for each pattern onto the thread.

Fig. 3a

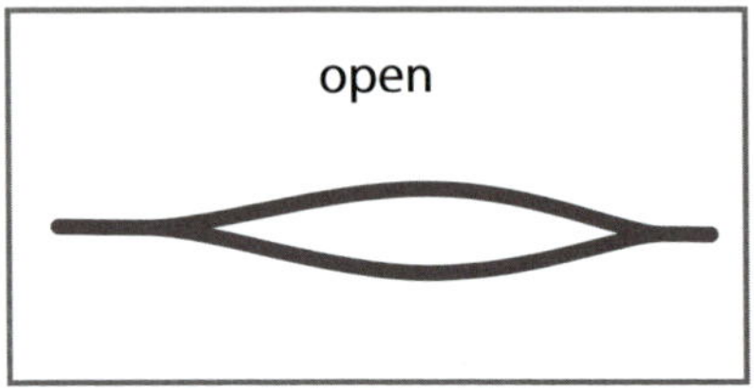

Fig. 3b

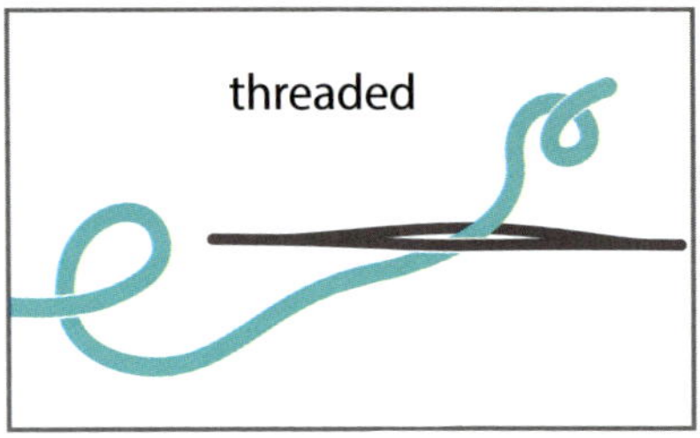

OVERHAND KNOT

Tie an overhand knot to secure strands ***(Fig. 4)***.

Fig. 4

Components

All components used in this book can be found in the beading/ jewelry section of any craft store.

Thread Information

The projects in this book were made using ***Aunt Lydia's® Classic Crochet Size 10™***, a Lace Weight thread. Any brand of Bedspread Weight (size 10) thread may be used.

For your convenience, listed below are the specific colors used to create our photography models. Because thread manufacturers make frequent changes in their product lines, you may sometimes find it necessary to use a substitute thread or to search for the discontinued product at alternate suppliers (locally or online).

BEADED NECKLACE & BRACELET
Teal - #0856 Peacock
Lt Green - #0397 Wasabi

CHAIN LINK NECKLACE
Burgundy - #0492 Burgundy
Aunt Lydia's® Classic Crochet Metallic Size 10™
Gold - #0090G Gold/Gold

ZIG-ZAG BRACELET
Pink - #0332 Hot Pink
Yellow - #0421 Goldenrod

FLOWER CUFF & EARRINGS
Olive - #0672 Olive
Orange - #0431 Pumpkin
Yellow - #0421 Goldenrod
Pink - #0332 Hot Pink
Lavender - #0119 Violet

CIRCLES & BEADS NECKLACE
#0250 Mexicana

MOTIF NECKLACE & EARRINGS
Lavender - #0495 Wood Violet
Lt Green - #0397 Wasabi

WOVEN BRACELET
Purple - #0458 Purple
Orange - #0431 Pumpkin
Aqua - #0451 Parakeet
Yellow - #0421 Goldenrod
Pink - #0332 Hot Pink

FAN PENDANT
Blue - #0805 Blue Hawaii
Lt Green - #0397 Wasabi

BEAD & TASSEL PENDANT
Purple - #0458 Purple
Olive - #0672 Olive
Orange - #0431 Pumpkin

Meet Edie Eckman

Years ago Edie Eckman co-owned a yarn shop. The work severely limited her time to knit and crochet, so she closed the shop after a while and turned to designing.

"Now I have my fingers in many aspects of the fiber arts," Edie says. She teaches her popular workshops at Stitches, the National Needlearts Association, Crochet Guild of America and The Knitting Guild of America conferences and other national venues, as well as at local shops and guilds. "I love the 'a-ha' moment when a student gains a new bit of understanding," she says.

When Edie wants to unplug from her fast-paced work life, she heads for the woods. "We have a little cabin. There's no TV or Internet service. I love to go there for walks and to paddle around the lake. However, I've always got designs in my head, ready to be sold."

To see Edie's workshop schedule, visit her Web site at EdieEckman.com. She can also be found on Facebook as EdieEckman, as well as on Ravelry.

We have made every effort to ensure that these instructions are accurate and complete. We cannot, however, be responsible for human error, typographical mistakes, or variations in individual work.

Production Team: Instructional/Technical Editor - Linda A. Daley; Senior Graphic Artist - Lora Puls; Graphic Artists; Amy L. Teeter and Victoria Temple; Photo Stylist - Lori Wenger; and Photographer - Jason Masters.

Made in U.S.A.